Patrick Mahomes

Patrick Mahomes

Mari Bolte

Living in THE SPOTLIGHT

CREATIVE EDUCATION
CREATIVE PAPERBACKS

Published by Creative Education and Creative Paperbacks
P.O. Box 227, Mankato, Minnesota 56002
Creative Education and Creative Paperbacks are imprints
of The Creative Company
www.thecreativecompany.us

Book design by Graham Morgan (www.bluedes.com)
Art direction by Tom Morgan

Images by Associated Press/AJ Mast, 19, Keith Gillett, 39, Kevin Sabitus, cover, Tim Warner, 10, Tony Gutierrez, 17; Getty Images/ANDREW CABALLERO-REYNOLDS, 45, Emily Curiel/Kansas City Star, 2, Jill Toyoshiba/Kansas City Star, 26, Kevin Winter, 46, LG Patterson, 36, PATRICK T. FALLON, 33, Rich Sugg/Kansas City Star, 34, Scott Winters/Icon Sportswire, 40–41, TIMOTHY A. CLARY, 9, 25; Wikimedia Commons/All-Pro Reels, cover, 6–7, 13, 20, 30, 43, 44, elisfkc2, 23, Larry Koester, 4–5, Moriah Levin, 14, U.S. Air National Guard Master Sgt. Michael Crane, 29

Library of Congress Cataloging-in-Publication Data
Names: Bolte, Mari author
Title: Patrick Mahomes / by Mari Bolte.
Description: Mankato, Minnesota : Creative Education and Creative Paperbacks, [2026] | Series: Living in the spotlight | Includes bibliographical references and index. | Audience: Ages 10-14 | Audience: Grades 7-9 | Summary: "Get to know football star Patrick Mahomes in this sports biography that showcases his Super Bowl wins with the Kansas City Chiefs, personal challenges, and off-field ventures. Written for middle-grade readers, it includes table of contents, sidebars, glossary, resources, and index"– Provided by publisher.
Identifiers: LCCN 2025021239 (print) | LCCN 2025021240 (ebook) | ISBN 9798895811290 library binding | ISBN 9798896800828 paperback | ISBN 9798895812556 ebook
Subjects: LCSH: Mahomes, Patrick, 1995–Juvenile literature | Kansas City Chiefs (Football team)–Juvenile literature | Quarterbacks (Football)–United States–Biography–Juvenile literature | Football players–United States–Biography–Juvenile literature | LCGFT: Biographies
Classification: LCC GV939.M284 B65 2026 (print) | LCC GV939.M284 (ebook) | DDC 796.332092 [B]–dc23/eng/20250609
LC record available at https://lccn.loc.gov/2025021239
LC ebook record available at https://lccn.loc.gov/2025021240

Printed in the United States

25
T. GRUNHARD
K. ANDERS
GO CHIEFS

15
65
NFL

CONTENTS

Introduction

On February 2, 2020, Hard Rock Stadium in Miami, Florida was packed with more than 62,400 fans, all of whom had gathered to watch Super Bowl LIV (54). Demi Lovato had sung the national anthem. The San Francisco 49ers were facing off against the Kansas City Chiefs. And Chiefs fans were hoping to see something they'd been denied the year before—a Super Bowl victory.

Chiefs quarterback Patrick Mahomes felt the pressure. The first three quarters of the game had been a struggle, and his team was down 20 to 10. Mahomes himself had run in a touchdown for the team's first six points. Throughout the season, he had overcome a dislocated knee, **turf toe**, and a **concussion**. Still, he led his team to their first Super Bowl appearance in 50 years. Kansas City wasn't about to let the 49ers have an easy victory.

During the fourth quarter, Mahomes threw the ball 141 yards. He connected with running back Damien Williams and tight end Travis Kelce for touchdowns to take the lead just before the game's final two minutes. The Chiefs defense stopped the 49ers from bouncing back. The final seconds ticked down. The game was over. Red and gold confetti spilled from the sky. The Kansas City Chiefs had won! Mahomes received the Super Bowl Most Valuable Player (MVP) Award. He was the youngest quarterback and third-youngest player to win Super Bowl MVP at 24 years, 138 days old. There would be many more record-breaking games to come.

NFL

Texas Tech University gave Mahomes the chance to play both baseball and football.

CHAPTER 1:

A Multi-Sport Athlete

Patrick Lavon Mahomes II was born on September 17, 1995, in Tyler, Texas, which is around 100 miles (161 km) from Dallas. His parents, Pat Mahomes Sr. and Randi Martin, had met after high school. They also had another son, Jackson, born in 2000.

Mahomes Sr. had played Major League Baseball (MLB) as a pitcher for the Minnesota Twins, Boston Red Sox, New York Mets, Texas Rangers, Chicago Cubs, and Pittsburgh Pirates before retiring in 2003. He also played for the Yokohama BayStars in Japan for a season and a half. The Mahomes family traveled along, attending spring training, regular games, and even the World Series. When the Mets made the World Series in 2000, Mahomes Sr. let his son catch fly balls in center field. He could bat, catch, and throw by the time he was three. A plastic bat and ball let young Mahomes have his own batting practices, even on the road.

Growing up, meeting professional athletes influenced Mahomes. His godfather was LaTroy Hawkins, a pitcher who played in the Major Leagues for 21 years. He played catch with baseball stars like Derek Jeter and Alex Rodriguez. "It made a huge impact on me...Just watching those guys and their work ethic but also seeing how good people they were." But traveling for work was hard on the Mahomes' marriage, and they divorced in 2006.

Young Mahomes played baseball, basketball, and football. He played golf and competed in the high jump. But baseball was his first love. With a strong, accurate throw and quick release, he could pitch a whole game with no problem. However, his powerful arm was too strong for T-ball. During his first practice at age six, Mahomes picked up a ground ball and threw it to the first baseman from shortstop. The kindergartener at first base wasn't ready. He took the ball to the face and his glasses shattered. Aside from that incident, Mahomes was a natural at shortstop. It's a position that requires flexibility and quick decision-making. He also played first base and outfield positions.

Basketball was his second favorite sport. But he wasn't tall enough to become a professional. Football came in at number three. Growing up in Texas, the Mahomes family watched the Dallas Cowboys and their quarterback Tony Romo. Mahomes was also a fan of Aaron Rodgers, Michael Vick, and Tom Brady. He started playing football in middle school and continued into high school. He was a safety and

Mahomes is a talented athlete in more than just football.

NFL
LH
15

ZOOM IN: PAT MAHOMES SR.

Pat Mahomes Sr. was a multi-sport athlete, playing baseball, football, and basketball in high school. He considered playing basketball in college but was drafted by the Minnesota Twins in the sixth round of the 1988 draft. He made his MLB debut in 1992, becoming part of the team's official starting rotation in 1994. He played professionally for 11 years, including a season and a half in Japan. Mahomes Sr. retired from the majors in 2003, playing for several minor and independent leagues. In 2007, he signed with the Sioux Falls Canaries. He played with them for two seasons, leading them to their first and only championship the next year. The Canaries inducted him to their Hall of Fame in 2019.

a quarterback. He still played his other favorite sports. Mahomes earned a starting point guard position on his high school basketball team during his freshman year. And he continued to build his baseball skills. To Mahomes, it didn't matter what the in-season sport was as long as he was on a winning team. He was going pro at one sport or another, and he was going to be the best.

Mahomes Sr. saw his son's potential for pro baseball. When Mahomes heard his dad's pitch topped out at 93 miles (150 kilometers) an hour, he worked hard until his own pitches reached speeds of 96 miles (155 km) per hour. After 10th grade, Mahomes's father encouraged his son to quit football to focus on his other dominant sports. "I just thought we were wasting time when he could have been working on the sports he would go to college for, baseball and basketball," said Mahomes Sr. "Plus, I didn't want him to get hurt." Mahomes had gained a lot of attention as a baseball player. During his senior year, he had a .450 batting average and had thrown a 16-strike no-hitter. He was ranked as the 35th-best MLB prospect in the whole state of Texas.

Being a triple threat at sports had a downside. Mahomes hadn't attended many of the elite football camps that would get him noticed by college recruiters. And because his high school already had an upperclassman in the starting quarterback position, Mahomes played as a safety his first two years. When he did go to football camps, he was placed in safety positions, even when he said he wanted to play quarterback. Mahomes didn't want to be a safety. He didn't like tackling. He wanted to lead the team. By the time he got the starting quarterback spot as a junior, he was ready for that role. During his senior year, he threw 4,619 yards and for 50 touchdowns. He also rushed for another 1,000 yards and was named the Male Athlete of the Year by high school rating website MaxPreps.

In 2014, the Detroit Tigers chose Mahomes in the 37th round of the MLB draft. But Mahomes wanted to play both baseball and football, and Texas Tech University in Lubbock, Texas, offered him that option. He would be a Red Raider, studying marketing while playing sports. He assumed he would play both sports for three years, and then give pro baseball a chance.

Unfortunately, college was different from high school. He couldn't give 50-50 attention to two sports. He gave football his full focus, because he was at Texas Tech on a football **scholarship**. It wasn't easy. During his freshman year, Mahomes spent most of the football season on the bench. His chance to shine came near the end of the season, after the starting quarterback got injured. He kept the role into his sophomore year. Eventually, Mahomes would rack up 11,252 passing yards and 93 career touchdowns. He also led the National Collegiate Athletics Association (NCAA) in yards per game, passing offense, and touchdowns. He even set an NCAA single-game passing yards record, with 734 total. ESPN ranked him as the number five quarterback prospect in the nation. In 2017, Mahomes **declared** for the National Football League (NFL) draft. He was ready to show the world what he could do.

ZOOM IN: BATTER UP

Football players being drafted into Major League Baseball isn't as uncommon as you would think! John Elway, Tom Brady, Jameis Winston, Kyler Murray, and Russell Wilson are only a few NFL stars who were drafted for baseball. Conversely, there are also MLB stars who gave up football, such as Bo Jackson, Joe Mauer, and Carl Crawford. Players can be drafted to the MLB when they're still in high school. However, they usually start in the minor leagues and may never actually make it to the majors. Players drafted by the NFL must be out of high school for at least three years.

Mahomes runs the 40-yard dash for the 2017 NFL Combine. He ran it in 4.8 seconds.

CHAPTER 2:

Making His Mark

Mahomes showed up at the 2017 NFL **Combine** ready to impress. He ran a 40-yard dash, did shuttle runs, three-cone drills, vertical jumps, and broad jumps. His skill for accurate throws and extending plays got some attention. But it was his brain that really impressed. When he visited with the Chiefs head coach, Andy Reid, a whiteboard of plays was set up. Reid showed Mahomes the plays before erasing them and asked him to recreate them. Mahomes had an **eidetic memory** and drew Reid's plays with no problem.

During the NFL draft, nine players were selected before Mahomes, including Mitch Trubisky, who was chosen as the Chicago Bears' future quarterback. The San Francisco 49ers were in need of a quarterback. So were the New Orleans Saints. Saints head coach Sean Payton had seen the potential in Mahomes.

YARD
DASH
10
QB

MAHOMES
15

ZOOM IN: THE PRO BOWL

The Pro Bowl is an NFL event that happens each year and is played between the Conference Championship game and the Super Bowl. It features the league's best players. Mahomes was first selected for the Pro Bowl in 2018 and has been every year since. Selections are **nominated** by and voted in by coaches, other players, and fans. Teams are made up of AFC and National Football Conference (NFC) players. Players who are going to the Super Bowl can be named to Pro Bowl teams, but don't play. Brady holds the record for most Pro Bowl nominations at 15.

Mahomes chose his old basketball jersey number, 15, as his number for the Chiefs.

They had the 11th pick in the first round. But the Chiefs weren't about to let that happen. They originally had the 27th pick, and knew that would be too late. So they traded the Buffalo Bills for the 10th pick, throwing in a third-round selection and a first-round pick in the 2017 draft. They got Mahomes!

Mahomes' first year was quiet. He mainly sat on the bench, watching starting quarterback Alex Smith. He took his first throw during the last regular-season game against the Denver Broncos. The Chiefs had won the division title the week before, clinching a playoff spot, so the 17th game of the season meant nothing except potential injuries for their starting players. Mahomes threw 284 yards for 22 of 33 completions and an interception. The game ended 28–24 with kicker Harrison Butker scoring the game-winning field goal. It was the first time since 1987 that a quarterback drafted by the Chiefs had claimed a victory for the team.

The next season, Smith was traded to the Washington Redskins (now the Washington Commanders) and Mahomes was given the starting position. His first game was against the Los Angeles Chargers. He threw for four touchdowns, earning an American Football Conference (AFC) best passer rating of 127.5. He was the fifth-youngest quarterback since 1970 to throw four or more touchdowns in a season-opening game. He was also only the sixth quarterback in Chiefs history to throw four or more touchdowns without an interception. The NFL named Mahomes the AFC Player of the Week. He won the title again the following week, and the AFC Offensive Player of the Month in September.

The season just kept getting better. After leading the NFL with 50 touchdown passes, Pro Football Writers of America named him the NFL's Most Valuable Player and the NFL's Offensive Player of the Year. The Chiefs finished the season 12–4, winning the AFC West. Their season ended at the AFC Championship, but it was an amazing start for their rookie quarterback. Mahomes had thrown for more than 5,000 yards, becoming the only quarterback in history to do that in both college and the NFL.

The 2019 season looked bright. The Chiefs won their first four games of the season. But in October, Mahomes dislocated his knee during a night game against the Denver Broncos. Doctors thought it would take three to six weeks to heal. Yet Mahomes was back at practice a week later. His flexibility, which made him such a valuable shortstop, protected the **ligaments** around his kneecap. For many, it would have been a more serious injury. He returned to the starting position in week 10 against the Tennessee Titans. The Chiefs lost, thanks to a last-second field goal attempt. But Mahomes was back. The Chiefs went on to win their division, the AFC Championship, and then Super Bowl LIV against the San Francisco 49ers. It was the team's first Super Bowl victory in 50 years.

In 2020, Mahomes signed a contract extension that kept him in Kansas City. At $450 million over 10 years, Mahomes would suit up in red and gold through 2031, with no risk of being traded. In total, with his already-existing rookie contract, **signing bonus**, and incentives, it was worth $503 million. Mahomes was the richest player in NFL history.

Even though the 2020 season was unusual due to the global pandemic, the Chiefs were ready for the challenge. Their entire preseason was canceled. But they easily won their first regular-season game against the Texans. Mahomes averaged nearly 30 points

Mahomes using his playmaking abilities against the Tampa Bay Buccaneers.

79
DAVID
54
HALL
90
62

game, and the team led the league in offensive yards and first downs. They finished 14–2, with the second loss coming from a final week 17 game with backup players on the field. Super Bowl LV (55) saw them meeting the Tampa Bay Buccaneers and their all-star quarterback, Brady. The Chiefs were unable to score a single touchdown, with Brady scoring three alone. In the end, the Chiefs lost 9-31.

The next season started out rocky, with an initial record of 3–4. But the team rallied. They won eight games in a row and earned a spot in the AFC Championship, which they lost to the Tampa Bay Buccaneers. The 2022 season sent them back to the Super Bowl, which they won thanks to a last-second field goal against the Philadelphia Eagles. Mahomes won his second MVP award and his second Super Bowl. Mahomes threw for 5,250 passing yards, making it his fifth-consecutive season over 4,000. Peyton Manning is the only other quarterback to have had such successful five-year spans in their first six years in the league.

ZOOM IN: SHUTTING DOWN

In March 2020, the country essentially closed because of the COVID-19 pandemic. Teams shut down their facilities to everyone but essential staff and players. The draft was done over Zoom. Free agents couldn't travel to interview with new teams. Offseason workouts were canceled, and teams spent thousands of dollars sending athletes equipment so they could exercise at home. Some games were canceled or rescheduled. Arrowhead Stadium in Kansas City was at just 22 percent capacity for safety. When vaccines became available, Mahomes and Coach Reid held a press conference to let the public know they had gotten them. Mahomes said protecting his infant daughter was his main motivator.

Mahomes proudly holds up his third Lombardi Trophy.

In October 2023, Mahomes threw his 200th career passing touchdown against the New York Jets. He was the fastest player in history to hit that milestone. A week later, he beat the Minnesota Vikings, becoming the youngest quarterback to best all 31 opposing teams. With an overtime Super Bowl victory over the 49ers, the Chiefs proved that they were still a leading power in the NFL. As for Mahomes, as of the 2024 season, he had led the Chiefs to five Super Bowl appearances. He won three (LIV, LVII, LVIII) and was named Super Bowl MVP each of those times.

15

CHAPTER 3:

It's Showtime

Mahomes' strong bond with his teammates is one of the secrets to his team's success. The 2018 offense was made up of mainly young players. Wide receiver Tyreek Hill had been drafted in 2016. Tight end Travis Kelce was a little older, drafted in 2013. Kelce found a leadership role on the team, boosting the confidence of the younger players.

With Mahomes in the quarterback spot, Hill and Kelce have had multiple seasons of 10 or more touchdowns and 1,000-plus yards. They were the third pair of teammates to hit these milestones over multiple seasons while playing for the same team. In 2024, Kelce and Mahomes set a touchdown record, with 16 between them. That surpassed the previous record set by Brady and Rob Gronkowski.

Mahomes and teammate Travis Kelce have one of the greatest connections in football.

Mahomes also has a strong bond with Coach Reid. Reid has given Mahomes lots of freedom to call plays or invent new ideas. This includes Mahomes' behind-the-back and no-look passes. While these passes started as a joke in college, the skill stemmed from

ZOOM IN: THE MAHOMES EFFECT

The Mahomes Effect plays a role on and off the field. His jersey has been a top seller since he started in the game. In 2020, he took the number-one spot on the player merchandise sales list. People didn't just buy jerseys. They got figurines, Hawaiian shirts, aprons, ornaments, and other items featuring Mahomes' face and name. In 2024, a Super Bowl-worn Mahomes jersey sold for $213,500. NFL jerseys aren't the only big sellers. Texas Tech has a line of Mahomes jerseys, hats, shoes, and other apparel with his name, number, and Gladiator logo. In 2024, the college added his personal logo to the Texas Tech team uniform.

his years playing basketball, where the turn of a guard's head can mean a clean throw to a receiver. But it's also a move that requires trust between the quarterback and the receiver. The receiver has to trust that the ball will get to them, even if it doesn't look like it's coming. Failure to run the route as discussed can lead to drops, misses, or even interceptions.

Not every play is successful. But Reid never tries to rein in his quarterback, and also takes inspiration from Mahomes in his own play calling. "I feel like Coach just kind of observes stuff Pat does during practice having fun and is like, 'Hmm, that could be pretty cool,'" former Chiefs offensive lineman Mitchell Schwartz said. Their relationship is seen in the team's success. Since Mahomes joined the league, no NFL team has won more games or scored more points.

Mahomes poses for a photo with service members for Military Appreciation Day.

15
NFL
LH
15
NFL

Mahomes' skill, discipline, and passion for football are what make him such a valuable player.

Talent, charisma, youth, and love of the game has been called The Mahomes Effect. His ability to create big plays means exciting games that draw in new fans. The Chiefs have a more than $993 million economic impact on Kansas City, through ticket sales, tourists, and football-related events. With four Super Bowl appearances since Mahomes joined the team, the Kansas City Chiefs are one of the most valuable NFL brands.

People are interested in seeing Mahomes play for many reasons—not just his unique moves. When the Chiefs played Jalen Hurts and the Philadelphia Eagles in Super Bowl LVII (57), it was the first time two Black starting quarterbacks had played each other. Mahomes has been outspoken about embracing his Black heritage. "I've learned more and more about the history of the Black quarterback since I've been in this league," he said. "I'm just glad we can set the stage for kids that are coming up now."

He has also attributed his throwing style to Negro League baseball players. Their creativity, skill, and love of their sport inspired him. He often visits the Negro League Baseball Museum in Kansas City. He has released a signature Adidas sneaker honoring the Kansas City Monarchs and has worn their jersey to Chiefs games. The Monarchs are a professional baseball team in the American Association of Professional Baseball, an MLB Partner League. They have a rich history, and were once a Negro League team.

Mahomes tends to focus on gameplay and stays out of any **controversy**. But that's not true for everyone in his family. In 2022, Mahomes married his high school sweetheart, Brittany. They have three children together. Mahomes' wife has a strong social media presence, with thousands of followers on X and Instagram. Since 2018, she has not shied away from speaking out against referee calls she felt went against the Chiefs. She has also been caught multiple times in negative interactions with fans and has been criticized for her political views.

Mahomes' brother has also had trouble in the spotlight. The younger Mahomes is an influencer who has been caught fighting with the public, dancing on the sidelines during a memorial dedicated to the late NFLer Sean Taylor, and crashing post-game interviews. In 2023, he was accused of assaulting two different people. A rumor that Mahomes' wife and brother were asked not to attend upcoming games spread in 2022; Mahomes seemed to deny it. Mahomes Sr. has had his own troubles as well. He has been charged for driving while impaired. He served 10 days in jail in 2024 after pleading guilty following his third arrest.

Despite family drama, Mahomes continues to focus on football. "It's a family matter, so I'll keep it to the family," he said after being asked about his father's arrest. "That's all I have to say." A little more than a week later, he led the team to a Super Bowl victory. If his mind was anywhere besides the game, no one would have known.

ZOOM IN: MEET THE MAHOMES FAMILY

Daughter Sterling Skye Mahomes (born in 2021) and son Patrick "Bronze" Lavon Mahomes III (born in 2022) are often spotted on the sidelines after Chiefs games. When Mahomes is on the road, the family stays in touch over FaceTime. Fans have enjoyed watching the children grow up over social media. Golden Raye was born on January 12, 2025. She attended her first Super Bowl at just three weeks old. The family theme of using precious metals as names dates back to their college days, when Brittany named her dog Steel. She thought about naming her second dog Sterling, but saved it for a daughter. They chose Silver for their dog instead.

Mahomes and his family at a post-Super Bowl LVIII (58) press conference

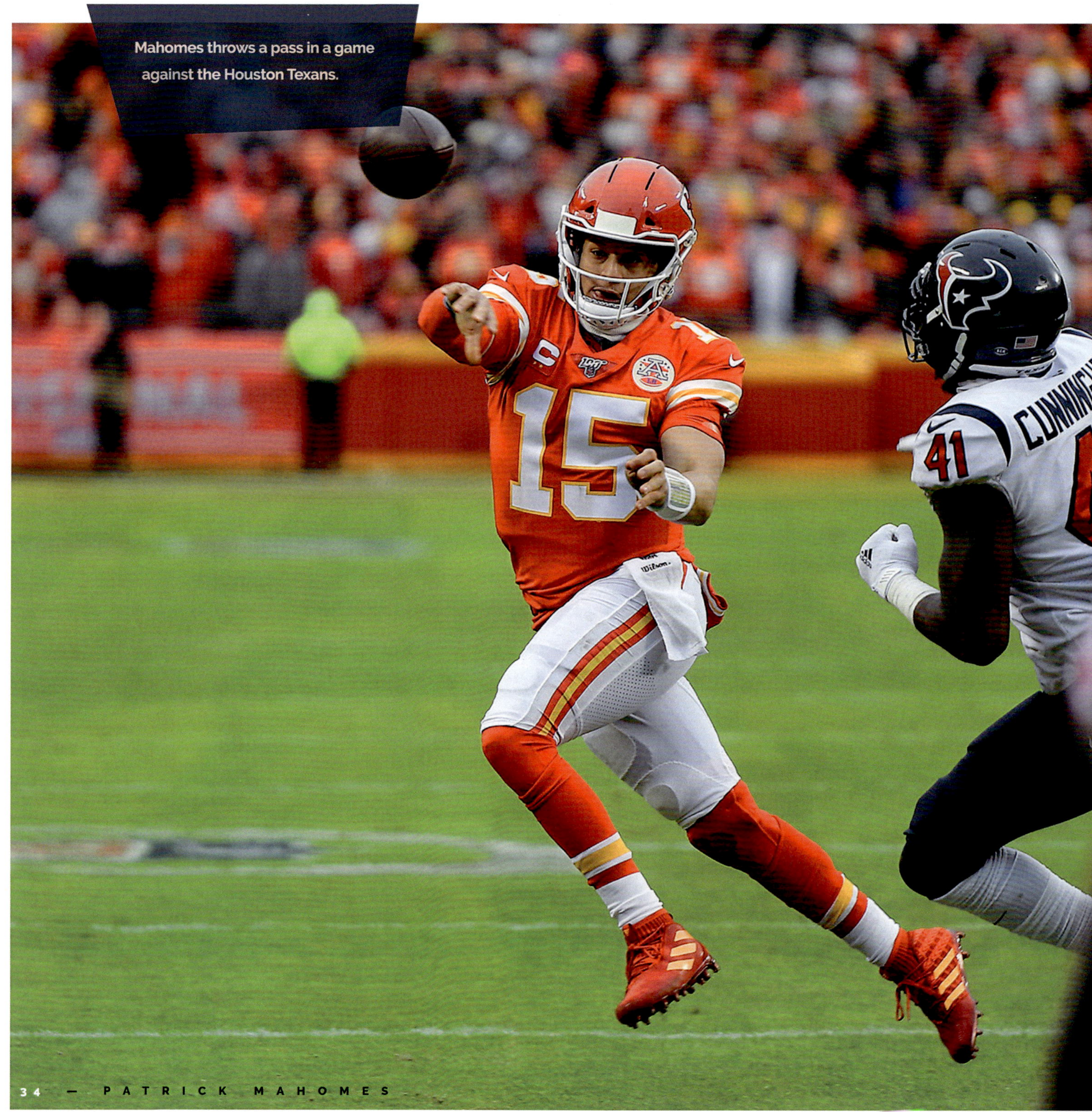

Mahomes throws a pass in a game against the Houston Texans.

CHAPTER 4:

This Is What I Do!

In 2023, Netflix subscribers got up-close and personal with the Mahomes family. The streaming service had partnered with the NFL to produce a docuseries called *Quarterback* that followed quarterbacks Mahomes, Kirk Cousins, and Marcus Mariota both on and off the field. They all wore microphones during each 2022 game, and Mahomes gave filmmakers special access to his life during the season. He recently formed a **production studio**, 2PM Productions, and helped produce the series, as well as its sequel program, *Receiver*.

Mahomes has used his fame to help others. In 2019, he founded 15 and the Mahomies Foundation, since 15 is his player number. Its signature program is called 15 for 15, which supports 15 youth

ZOOM IN: GALVANIZED BY 2PM

Friends gave Mahomes the 2PM nickname because he's Patrick Mahomes II. The logo he uses is a gladiator mask. Mahomes said it "represents the mindset of making an impact every single day. Whether it's training in the gym, on-field practice or a game day—that's always my mentality." For a time, the logo was exclusive to Texas Tech's special football uniforms (also known as the Mahomes Strategy Uniform). By 2024, it was seen on the football team's regular uniforms as well. "Seeing my own logo on the Texas Tech uniform I put so much blood, sweat, and tears in is one of the most meaningful off-field accomplishments of my career," said Mahomes.

Mahomes works with players for the Kansas City MLB Urban Youth Academy.

charities. Volunteer for 15 encourages kids ages 11 to 18 to volunteer 15 hours or more in their community. In 2024, around 2,000 youths gave 80,000 hours of volunteer time. Read for 15 awards kids and parents for committing to read 15 minutes a day for 15 weeks. In 2024, 15 and the Mahomies donated $1,500 for every touchdown Mahomes scored, with a goal of $50,000 during the year and $1.625 million over multiple years. The organization also awarded $615,000 in grants to 19 different charitable organizations. An annual gala brings together hundreds of supporters. In 2024, $1,077,000 was raised by 850 attendees. Four tickets to Taylor Swift's Eras Tour went for $80,000 alone.

Mahomes didn't **endorse** a presidential candidate in 2024, but he was in ads to encourage voter registration. He, Kelce, and players from the Kansas City Royals baseball team also encouraged voters to vote "yes" on whether tax money should be used to fund a new baseball stadium and a renovation at the Truman Sports Complex, where the Chiefs practice. Mahomes was more than a little interested in the future of the Royals. In 2020, he became a part owner of the team. He also invested in the city's Major League Soccer (MLS) team, Sporting Kansas City. His wife is a co-owner of the city's National Women's Soccer League (NWSL) team, the Kansas City Current.

People associate Mahomes with football and baseball, but he has another interest—pickleball! He and Kelce invested in restaurant-and-pickleball-court chain called Chicken N Pickle. The two also opened a steakhouse called 1587 Prime together and were joint investors in the fast-food chain Whataburger. And, going beyond food and field sports, Kelce and Mahomes led a new investment group to fund Alpine F1, a Formula One racing team. It was a fitting investment—the Netflix show *Drive to Survive* was what inspired Mahomes to participate in *Quarterback*.

Kansas City has professional football, baseball, men's soccer, and women's soccer. Women's basketball is the next natural step. Mahomes was impressed with how the KC Current's ownership team handled introducing professional women's sports to the city. "Kansas City is such a great place for me," he said. "I think being involved in the community [is important], and I love sports. I know how much the city loves sports, so let's bring as many sports in here and showcase how great Kansas City is not only as a city, but the people that are in the city as well." He said he wants his daughters to be able to follow their own dreams when they're old enough. And growing women's sports is key.

No matter how famous he gets, Mahomes hasn't forgotten his **alma mater**. In 2024, he donated $5 million to the school's stadium renovation fund. The walkthrough area of the football center, the quarterback meeting room, and the offensive coordinator's office will be named after Mahomes.

The future looks bright for Mahomes and the Chiefs. In 2023, his record-breaking contract was restructured to pay him $210.6 million through 2026, the most in history over four years. With

ZOOM IN: AN INSPIRING HERITAGE

Baseball became popular after the Civil War. Black Americans were barred from playing at the highest levels so they organized their own teams. In 1920, the Negro National League (NNL) was formed. Hundreds of thousands of fans gathered to watch legends like Josh Gibson, Satchel Paige, and Turkey Stearns. The Great Depression nearly saw the end of the NNL, but it rose again in 1933 with the founding of the Negro American League. In 1944, Negro League star Jackie Robinson became the first Black player in Major League Baseball. He paved the way for Black baseball players in America and inspired other Black athletes, too.

Mahomes was honored with a specialty Kansas City Royals (MLB) jersey.

15
C
NFL
LH
15

Mahomes is one of the greatest NFL players we will see for many years to come.

bonuses, the total payout could reach $218.1 million. He went into the 2024 season on the tail of Len Dawson as the Chief's leader in passing yards and touchdown passes. He was set up to be the fastest to reach 30,000 passing yards, to surpass Peyton Manning's most touchdown passes by a player in his first eight seasons, and to achieve the title of fastest to reach 250 passing touchdowns.

Success doesn't come without failure. On February 9, 2025, the Chiefs were defeated during Super Bowl LIX (59). The Philadelphia Eagles beat them 40–22. Fans around the country were shocked. The Chiefs had been favored to win. People had wondered for weeks if they would see Mahomes lead the team to the NFL's first "three-peat." And it hadn't happened.

The future looks bright for Mahomes and the Chiefs. In 2023, his record-breaking contract was restructured to pay him $210.6 million through 2026, the most in history over four years.

A visibly upset Mahomes was seen both on the field and in the locker room after the game. But he took responsibility for the loss. "They played better than us from start to finish," he said. He acknowledged that the interceptions that had given the Eagles 14 points were his fault. But he vowed to play better. He apologized to fans online. And he showed the world that the Chiefs weren't about to give up.

Mahomes spent the 2025 off-season working out. Fans immediately noticed a difference. The Chiefs also took seven new players during that year's NFL draft and picked up another 13 after the draft closed. Building up their offensive line would give Mahomes time to complete the scoring drives the Chiefs had gotten used to seeing.

There are many more records Mahomes could still beat. The biggest is Brady's "impossible" record. Brady threw for 89,214 passing yards during his career. Mahomes ended the 2024-25 season with 32,352 yards. Brady's record was earned over 335 games in 23 seasons. Mahomes is still in the single digits.

Regardless of when he retires, he will go down as one of the best quarterbacks in NFL history.

Highlight Reel

DON'T BLINK

Mahomes is famous for his no-look pass. During a 2018 game against the Baltimore Ravens, he avoided being tackled while dodging left, then right. While keeping his face pointed forward, he threw the ball diagonally across his body to Demarcus Robinson, who was waiting 17 yards down the left side of the field. Mahomes had avoided taking a sack and the Chiefs continued their drive down the field. Viewers were in awe of the daring and flawless move. Long-time football fans familiar with the Texas Tech alum weren't surprised, though. He had been doing the move for years. "[Mahomes] does all those no-look things," Coach Reid said in an interview. "Those are the things that people go, 'Whoa.' He did it in college and then you go, 'Well, that's college. We'll see if he can do it here'… And then he did it here, in practice; he did it in a game at Denver; and now you just think he can do it." Mahomes insists that he doesn't intend on throwing no-look passes. They just happen out of instinct. And they are frustrating for both opponents and teammates. During Mahomes' rookie season, he tried it at practice against the Chief's first-team defense, looking straight downfield while throwing at a slant. It worked over and over, frustrating defenders who weren't expecting the ball to be thrown behind them. Jordan Love, Zach Wilson, and Bryce Young are all quarterbacks who may owe Mahomes for showing teams to look outside the box.

THE DANGEROUS PARADE

Kansas City planned a huge parade after the Chiefs won the Super Bowl in 2024. They had held similar parades in 2020 and 2023. More than a million people had attended the 2023 parade. Additional crowds were expected. Right at 11 a.m. the Chiefs kicked off the parade. Players waved from tall, double-decker buses and open-top SUVs that proclaimed the Chief's back-to-back Super Bowl Championships. They were joined by coaches, family members, staff, and mascots. Other players walked the route, giving high-fives and posing for selfies. Red and gold confetti flew through the air. Suddenly, an argument broke out between two strangers, 23-year-old Lyndell Mays and 18-year-old Dominic Miller. People at the parade had begun backing away from the fight. Then, Mays began shooting. Bullets flew through the air and ricocheted off the ground, hitting innocent bystanders. In response, others pulled their own weapons. In total, a dozen people brandished firearms—including two AR-15-style guns and two that were illegally purchased—and at least six fired them. One person, 43-year-old radio DJ Lisa Lopez-Galvan, was killed by a bullet from Miller's gun. Another 22 people, more than half of them under the age of 16, were wounded.

In the shooting's aftermath, the Chiefs partnered with the United Way to create an emergency fund called KC Strong. Mahomes and the 15 and the Mahomies Foundation personally donated $50,000. He also urged people to make their own donations if they could. The money supported victims and their families, first responders, violence prevention, and mental health services.

MAN OF THE YEAR

The NFL Man of the Year was first awarded in 1970. It was given to players who display excellence on and off the field. Character, philanthropy, and a commitment to society are important in this choice. Each team nominates a player. The winner is announced before the Super Bowl. They are given a trophy and a badge or helmet decal they can wear the rest of their career, if they're still active players. An additional $250,000 donation to their charity of choice is also part of the prize. In 1999, the award was renamed the Walter Payton Man of the Year in honor of Walter Payton, a beloved running back. He played for the Chicago Bears his entire 13-year NFL career, from 1975 to 1987. During that time, he set a number of records and was inducted into the Pro Football Hall of Fame in 1993. In February 1999, Payton shared that he had a rare liver disease and liver cancer. Payton used the last few months of his life to encourage people to consider organ donation. Illinois had a 25-percent increase in registered organ donors after Payton's public service announcement. The Walter Payton Man of the Year award is one of the NFL's highest individual honors. Mahomes was nominated in both 2022 and 2023 and won in 2023. He joined just a handful of others to win both Man of the Year and the NFL MVP Award.

Glossary

alma mater—the college or university someone attended

combine—the NFL scouting combine is a chance for college players to show off their skills to NFL scouts, general managers, and coaches

concussion—a temporary brain injury caused by impact to the head

controversy—a lot of discussion or debate about a topic

declared—when an athlete officially announces that they want to be chosen by a professional team in the upcoming draft

drafted—when a team signs a player to a contract

eidetic memory—when someone can remember exact images, sounds, or objects after only seeing it briefly

endorse—to publicly support or approve

free agents—athletes who don't have a contract and can play for any team

ligaments—tissue that connects two bones together

nominated—suggesting someone for a role or honor

production studio—when a company is set up to help make and distribute content like movies and shows

scholarship—financial aid to help students pay for school

signing bonus—a payment offered to someone to get them to accept a job

turf toe—when the big toe joint gets sprained

Selected Bibliography

15 and the Mahomies https://www.15andthemahomies.org/

Dent, Mark. *Kingdom Quarterback: Patrick Mahomes, the Kansas City Chiefs, and How A Once Swingin' Cow Town Chased the Ultimate Comeback*. New York: Dutton, 2023.

Florio, Mike. *Playmakers: How the NFL Really Works (And Doesn't).* New York: PublicAffairs, 2022.

Kansas City Chiefs: Patrick Mahomes https://www.chiefs.com/team/players-roster/patrick-mahomes/

Reid, Jason. *Rise of the Black Quarterback: What it Means for America*. Los Angeles: Andscape, 2022.

Roland, James. *Next Generation: NFL Star Quarterbacks*. San Diego, CA: ReferencePoint Press, 2025.

Websites

Britannica Kids: Patrick Mahomes
https://kids.britannica.com/students/article/Patrick-Mahomes/632146
Patrick Mahomes biography

Learn more about Patrick Mahomes, his family, and his career.
Chiefs Kingdom: Kids
https://www.chiefs.com/kids/
Join the Chiefs fan club, open to kids 12 and under.

Index